JESSE JAMES

JOHN ERNST
Maps by Theodore Miller

Prentice-Hall, Inc.
Englewood Cliffs, N.J.

For Alexandra and Matthew

Printed in the United States of America   .J

Prentice-Hall International, Inc., London
Prentice-Hall of Australia, Pty. Ltd., North Sydney
Prentice-Hall of Canada, Ltd., Toronto
Prentice-Hall of India Private Ltd., New Delhi
Prentice-Hall of Japan, Inc., Tokyo
Prentice-Hall of Southeast Asia Pte. Ltd., Singapore

10 9 8 7 6 5 4 3 2 1

Library of Congress Cataloging in Publication Data

Ernst, John, 1940-
    Jesse James.

    SUMMARY: Biography of Jesse James which examines his exploits in light of nineteenth-century society and politics.
    1. James, Jesse Woodson, 1847-1882—Juvenile literature.
[1. James, Jesse Woodson, 1847-1882.
2. Robbers and outlaws] I. Title.
F594.J2813   364.1'55'0924 [B] [92] 76-10206
ISBN 0-13-509695-2

CONTENTS

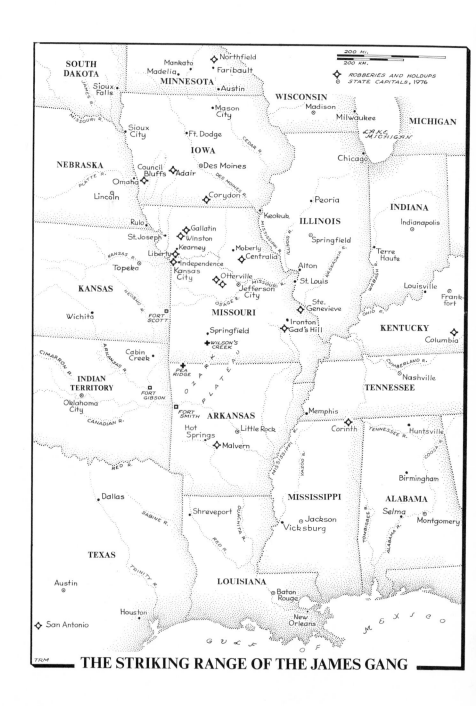

THE STRIKING RANGE OF THE JAMES GANG

CHAPTER ONE

The Liberty Raid

On February 13, 1866 twelve armed men drifted into the town of Liberty, Missouri, riding in twos and threes. They met in the main square, opposite the Clay County Savings Association—a squat, two-story brick structure with arched doorways and a peaked roof. This was their target.

Two of the men entered the bank. It was early morning, and Greenup Bird, the cashier, and his son, William, who was a bookkeeper, were preparing for the day's business. One of the strangers asked to have a bill changed. But when William Bird rose to make change, the man drew a six-shooter and ordered him to open the vault. The Birds did as they were told, and the robbers stuffed $60,000 in valuables into a wheat sack they were carrying. Finally, they herded the cashier and his son into the empty vault and shut the door.

The story goes that one of the outlaws said to Greenup Bird: "All birds should be caged. Get inside the vault, Mr. Bird, and step lively." It was the kind of joke that was typical of Jesse James.

The robbers left the sack of money on the bank doorstep for their confederates to pick up, while they mounted their horses. Inside the vault the two Birds realized that the spring lock had not

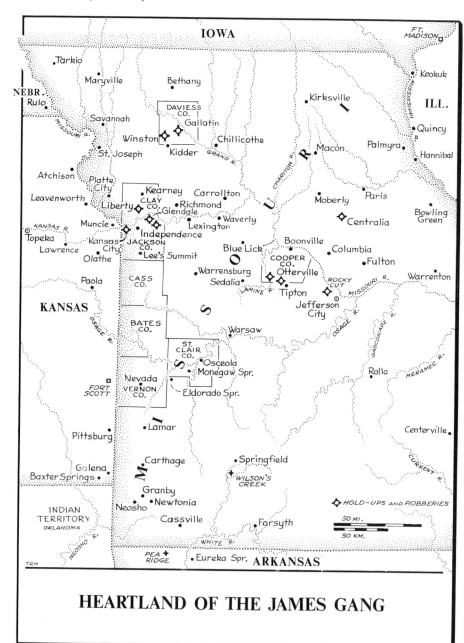

HEARTLAND OF THE JAMES GANG

clicked in place. They pushed open the door and rushed out, shouting the alarm.

The gang raced up and down the town square on horseback, yelling war cries and firing their pistols. One stroller who did not get off the street quickly enough was George Wymore, a nineteen-year-old student at nearby William Jewell College. Wymore was shot and killed.

The twelve bandits rode out of town, still whooping and firing their weapons. They headed north, then swung south toward the Missouri River, which they crossed by ferry. The posse organized to pursue them lost the trail in a fierce snowstorm. Although a reward was offered, none of the stolen money was ever returned, nor were any of the outlaws captured.

As a result of the robbery, the Clay County Savings Association went out of business. The building was later used to house a hat shop.

No one knows for sure whether Jesse James was one of the men who held up the Liberty bank. There are those who say that Jesse was at home in Kearney, twelve miles away, recovering from a gunshot wound, on the day of the robbery. A witness who claimed to recognize Jesse and his older brother, Frank, as they rode out of Liberty later changed his story. What we do know is that the members of the Liberty gang were friends of the James brothers who fought alongside them during the Civil War. It is also certain that many of these same men joined Jesse and Frank on future raids in which the plan of attack was strikingly similar.

Whether or not Jesse and Frank were among the twelve at Liberty, this daring hold-up set a grim pattern. It was the first daylight raid by an organized gang ever to be staged during peacetime.

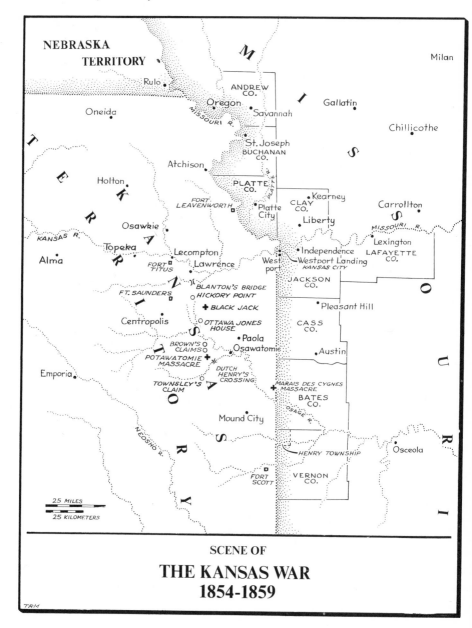

SCENE OF

THE KANSAS WAR
1854-1859

CHAPTER TWO

Clay County Beginnings

Robert James and Zerelda Cole met in Kentucky. Robert was studying to be a preacher, and Zerelda was attending a convent school. Shortly afterward, they were married. He was twenty-three. She was seventeen. Strangely enough, this deeply religious young couple became the parents of the most notorious outlaw brothers in America.

In 1842, the year after their marriage, the Jameses moved from Kentucky to Missouri. They settled on a farm near Kearney, and Robert James began preaching on Sundays in the New Hope Baptist Church. His congregation soon grew, and he helped establish two other Baptist churches. He also helped start William Jewell College in Liberty, the college Jolly Wymore had been attending when he was shot dead in the street.

Four children were born to the Jameses: Alexander Franklin (Frank) James in 1843, a boy who died as a baby in 1845, Jesse Woodson James on September 5, 1847, and a girl, Susan, in 1849.

The year Susan was born, gold was discovered in California. The news crackled through the country like an electric current. Although Robert James was doing well in Missouri, he decided to make the long journey to the gold fields. According to family legend, Jesse, who was two years old, clung to his father's legs and begged him not to go. But Robert James had spent a great deal of money preparing for the trip and had given his word to the other members of the party. He had little choice but to go. Eighteen days after he arrived in California, Robert James became sick and died. He was buried in an unmarked grave.

A year later Zerelda James, left alone with three young children, married a neighbor, Benjamin Simms. The two soon separated, probably because Simms did not get along with the James children. He died shortly after the separation.

Zerelda James married for a third time in 1855. Her new husband was Reuben Samuel, a doctor from Kentucky. Zerelda James Samuel was a spitfire of a woman with strongly-held ideas and a fierce devotion to her children. Dr. Samuel was an entirely different sort. Mild and easy-going, he became, in his own quiet way, deeply attached to his step-children and remained loyal to them for the rest of his life. The combination of two such different personalities seems to have worked, and the marriage held together through terrible strains.

The years during which Jesse James was growing up on the old James farm near the Missouri-Kansas border were scarred by trouble. The main cause of the trouble was the question of slavery. Missourians, many of whom (including Zerelda Samuel) came from the South, tended to be in favor of slavery. The Samuels themselves were slaveowners.

When Kansas, just across the Missouri River, was opened for settlement in 1854, Congress decided that the people of Kansas should determine whether or not slavery would be allowed in the new territory. This set the scene for the vicious border fighting that followed. Many Northerners who opposed slavery hoped to establish Kansas as a free state, where slavery would be forbidden. Packing up their belongings, they flooded into the territory. As pro-slavery Missourians watched uneasily from across the river, the Northerners staked out more and more land. Eventually fighting broke out on both sides of the river. Bands of anti-slavery Kansans, known as Jayhawkers or Redlegs, raided farms in Missouri, burning, looting, and carrying off slaves to set them free. Missourians, sometimes called Bushwackers or Border Ruffians, invaded Kansas to re-capture slaves, to terrorize settlers from the North, and to vote illegally in Kansas elections, hoping to swell the pro-slavery count. The toll of killings mounted. To be on one side of the issue or another became enough reason to be shot in the back on a lonely road.

Clay County, where Jesse grew up, was one of the border areas in which the fighting was bitterest. Jesse was undoubtedly aware of it when he was still young. Boys in the border counties often played a game in which they hung or shot at dummies made up to look like John Brown, a famous anti-slavery leader. In another game they "hunted down" a friend who pretended to be Jim Lane, a Kansas free-state spokesman. Some of them had witnessed shootings or even had members of their families killed. Early on they learned that violence was a way of life along the border.

But there was also a peaceful side to life in western Missouri during the middle of the last century. Both Jesse and Frank had chores to do on the farm. Zerelda Samuel maintained firm religious beliefs, and the family attended church regularly. All three of the James children went to Sunday school, where they read the Bible and sang hymns. Neither Jesse nor Frank ever completely forgot this early religious training.

Although it was a slave state, Missouri did not secede from the Union when the Civil War broke out, and during the early years of the war, pro- and anti-slavery factions struggled for control. At the age of eighteen Frank James signed up on the Southern side and took part in the savagely-fought battle of

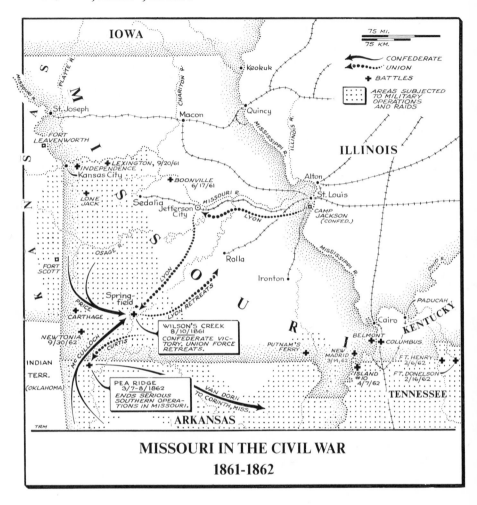

**MISSOURI IN THE CIVIL WAR
1861-1862**

Wilson's Creek, which the South won. While on a visit home after the battle, his outspoken support of the Southern cause got him into trouble. He was jailed by anti-slavery militia—groups of armed citizens organized to defend their home territory against rebels—and was released only after he signed a paper saying that he would never again engage in combat against the Federal Government.

Instead, Frank joined up with William C. Quantrill, the leader of a band of guerrillas fighting for the South. The guerrillas were not a part of the regular army. They wore no uniforms and recognized none of the rules of warfare. Captured Northerners could expect no mercy from them, and each of Quantrill's men knew that if he were taken by the enemy, he would be shot.

Frank's guerrilla activities and his family's sympathy for the South brought violence to the James-Samuel farm. One day in June, 1863 a squad of anti-slavery militia rode onto the Samuels' land. The soldiers accused Dr. Samuel of being disloyal to the Federal Government and of hiding guerrilla troops. They bound his hands behind his back, strung a rope around his neck, and slung the rope over a branch of a coffee tree. Then they yanked on the rope until Dr. Samuel was hanging by his neck, both feet off the ground, gasping for breath. They lowered him and hauled him up again several times. Finally, they tied the end of the rope to the tree trunk and left him dangling there, choking. Zerelda Samuel saved her husband by cutting him down as soon as the soldiers were out of sight.

But the militiamen had not left the farm. They had gone looking for Jesse. Knowing Frank was fighting with the guerrillas, they decided to show Jesse what could happen to Southern sympathizers.

The militia troops found Jesse working in a corn field. They drove him through the rows, lashing his back with a rope until it was criss-crossed with bloody welts that stuck to his shirt.

Hurt and humiliated and furious, Jesse was determined to strike back. He volunteered for Quantrill's band but was turned away because he was only fifteen. When word got around that he had been to see Quantrill, the militia returned to the Samuel farm. Neither Jesse nor his step-father were at home, but Zerelda

Samuel was there. And so was twelve-year-old Susie. Both were jailed as Southern sympathizers for several weeks.

More impatient than ever to get into combat, Jesse finally managed to sign up with "Bloody" Bill Anderson, one of Quantrill's lieutenants. At last he was in the war. Not long afterward, Anderson was to say of him: "For a beardless boy, he is the keenest and cleanest fighter in the command."

CHAPTER THREE

Guerrilla Fighter

At seventeen, Jesse James was slim and boyish-looking, with an oval face and pale blue eyes. It was the eyes that people noticed: something about them caught and held attention. As a result of a childhood disease Jesse blinked often. The effect was like that of a strong light snapping off and on.

Jesse had one other unusual physical feature. He was missing the tip of the middle finger of his left hand. After becoming an outlaw, he wore gloves so that he could not be identified by the disfigured hand. The story goes that he lost the finger tip shortly after he had joined the guerrillas. Jesse was cleaning a pistol, and it fired accidentally. Supposedly Jesse stared at the wounded finger in a puzzled way, then exclaimed: "Isn't that the dingest darndest thing!" The seasoned guerrillas, accustomed to much harsher language, were highly amused and began calling Jesse "Dingus."

Not long after volunteering for Bill Anderson's band, Jesse nearly died. In August, 1864, about sixty-five of Anderson's men were attacked by a much larger force of Federal troops and Kansas Redlegs at Flat Rock Ford. The guerrillas, outgunned and taken by surprise, suffered a number of casualties before they were able to get away. Jesse was hit in the right side of the chest.

It was a bad wound, so bad that he was not expected to live. But Jesse was young and strong, and he was soon well enough to re-join the guerrillas.

That September, Jesse and his brother Frank joined over two hundred guerrillas under the command of Anderson and George Todd camped in the woods near Centralia. On the morning of the 27th, Bill Anderson led a small raiding party into Centralia. The guerrillas took over the town, burned the railroad station and robbed the passengers of an incoming stage coach. At midday a train arrived from the east. It was stopped by railroad ties that Anderson's men had laid across the tracks. Firing warning shots, Anderson and his men rounded up the passengers and forced them off the train. As it happened, there were two dozen Northern soldiers in the group. These men were ordered to take off their uniforms, which the guerrillas could use as disguises. Then they were shot. Only one man was spared, either because he was an officer or because Anderson needed a prisoner to exchange for a captured Southerner. Before leaving town Anderson set fire to the train and sent it hurtling down the tracks with an open throttle, out of control.

It is said that Anderson tied a knot in a silk cord he carried with him for each Union soldier he killed. At the time of his death there were fifty-four knots in the cord. To most Northerners, Anderson seemed a blood-crazed madman; to many Southerners, he was a hero. Anderson did have a personal reason for hating Union men. His sister, along with three other women, had died in the collapse of a jail where she was being held prisoner by Federal forces. Anderson believed that the Northerners had purposely weakened the supports of the building, causing the collapse.

The day of the Centralia massacre, as the slaughter of Union soldiers became known, Northern troops led by Major A.V.E. Johnson pursued the guerrillas to their camp. Johnson commanded a large mounted force, but instead of charging on horse-

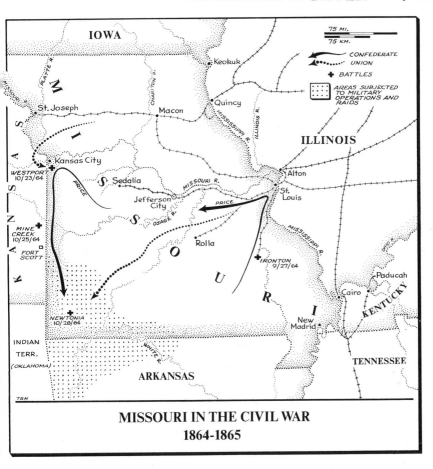

75 MI.
75 KM.

⟵ CONFEDERATE
◂•••••▸ UNION

✚ BATTLES

⬚⬚⬚ AREAS SUBJECTED
⬚⬚⬚ TO MILITARY
OPERATIONS AND
RAIDS

IOWA

Keokuk

St. Joseph

Macon

Quincy

MISSOURI

ILLINOIS

Kansas City

Alton

WESTPORT
10/23/64

Sedalia

PRICE

MISSOURI R.

St.
Louis

Jefferson
City

PRICE

MINE
CREEK
10/25/64

Rolla

FORT
SCOTT

IRONTON
9/27/64

Paducah

Cairo

KENTUCKY

NEWTONIA
10/28/64

New
Madrid

INDIAN
TERR.

(OKLAHOMA)

TENNESSEE

ARKANSAS

TRM

**MISSOURI IN THE CIVIL WAR
1864-1865**

back, he and his men dismounted. It was a disastrous mistake. The guerrillas were well-drilled horsemen. The animals they rode were the finest in the region. Anderson's men could shoot a pistol from either hand while riding at a dead run, holding the reins between their teeth. And they were desperate. They could not afford to be captured.

The guerrillas attacked Johnson's unmounted cavalrymen at a gallop. They came like a hurricane. They came like a river of fire. Within minutes the battle was over. Only a handful of Johnson's men escaped alive. Jesse himself is credited with having killed Major Johnson. In all, the Union force lost well over a hundred men; the guerrillas lost three.

That was one of the last victories for the guerrillas. The long, terrible war was drawing to a close. During the next few weeks both Anderson and Todd were killed, and the Confederate army retreated from Missouri, leaving the guerrillas without support. Pressed hard by Union troops, the guerrillas scattered. Frank James went to Kentucky with his old commander, Quantrill. But when Quantrill, too, was killed, Frank surrendered. He was allowed to return home after promising for the second time never again to take up arms against the Federal government.

Jesse spent the winter of 1864–65 in Texas. The following spring he returned to Missouri with a small band of guerrilla veterans. By this time the Confederacy had fallen. The war was over.

Jesse and his party were riding toward Lexington, under a white flag of truce, intending to surrender, when they met a force of Union soldiers. One or both sides opened fire. Jesse was hit in the chest and tumbled from the saddle. His horse, also hit, fell on top of him. Somehow Jesse managed to pull himself clear and run for cover chased by Union soldiers. Turning to fire, he killed the lead soldier's horse, gaining time to escape. Jesse wrenched off his boots, which were now full of blood from his wound, and ran on until he collapsed at the edge of a stream.

All that night Jesse lay by the stream, washing his wound and drinking the cool streamwater to ease his fever. Then he stumbled out to a field, where he was found by a farm worker who happened to be plowing nearby. His ordeal was over.

CHAPTER FOUR

Horse and Revolver Work

While Jesse was at war, his mother and step-father had been driven from their farm by the militia. Many Missourians who sided with the South had lost their homes and were forced to move to other areas. The Samuel family settled in Rulo, Nebraska, near the Missouri border. When Jesse had recovered sufficiently from his wound, he boarded a steamboat at Lexington and sailed up the Missouri River to join the Samuels in their Nebraska exile.

Jesse remained in Nebraska for about two months. He was still weak and sick, and he did not seem to be getting any better. At last he said to Zerelda: "Ma, I don't want to be buried up here in a Northern state." Though it was dangerous for them to return to Missouri so soon after the war, the family packed up and started downriver toward home.

On the way, they stopped at a boarding house run by Jesse's aunt, Mrs. John Mimms. Her daughter, named Zerelda after Jesse's mother, helped to care for Jesse, who was too weak to leave his bed. During the next four months Jesse gradually gained back some of his strength. At the same time he and his pretty cousin began to realize that they loved each other. By fall, when he was well enough to be carried in a wagon to the Samuel farm, Jesse and Zee, as he nicknamed her, were engaged to be married. It was not until nine years later that the wedding ceremony took place, but Jesse and Zee kept in touch during all that time, and their affection for each other survived the long separations.

Back home, Jesse slowly recovered, although his wound continued to re-open from time to time. When it did, he had to drain large amounts of puss from his chest. Jesse and Frank lived on the Samuel farm and worked in the fields. Jesse joined the choir of the local Baptist church and was baptized there. The family began to have a normal life again.

But the bitterness of the war years spilled over into peacetime. The James brothers lived in a state controlled by their former enemies. Missouri's constitution did not allow former Confederates to practice law, medicine, or other professions. They were not even allowed to serve as officers of a church. Furthermore, although ex-Union soldiers were pardoned for all wartime activities, Confederate veterans were not pardoned and could be jailed for crimes committed during the war.

For a time Missouri was a lawless wasteland. There were ambushes. There were lynchings. Armed horsemen prowled the state in packs, robbing and killing. Although some ex-guerrillas settled down to become peaceful citizens, others took up their weapons again, determined to earn their livings with a gun.

In February, 1866, while Jesse was still weak from his wound, six members of the local militia surrounded the Samuels' farmhouse in the middle of a bitterly cold moonlit night. One of them knocked on the door, waking Jesse, who looked out the window and saw six horses with U.S. Army saddles standing in the snow. Alerted, he dressed quickly and picked up his guns. The man at the door demanded that he come out, but Dr. Samuel stalled until Jesse was ready. There was no thought of giving himself up to be charged with war crimes. As he later told a friend: "Surrender had played out for good for me." Jesse fired a shot through the door, then pulled it open and burst outside.

Taken by surprise, the militiamen backed off, and Jesse was able to reach his horse and escape.

Eventually, Jesse decided to leave home, either for reasons of health, or to avoid further harassment from night riders. He went to New York City, then boarded a ship bound by way of Panama for California, joining Frank at the home of their uncle, Woodson James, in Paso Robles. There the two brothers rested and soaked in the nearby sulphur baths. Not until a year later did they return to the Samuel farm.

❀ ❀ ❀

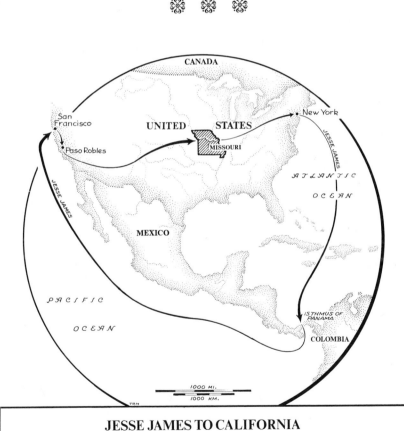

JESSE JAMES TO CALIFORNIA
1866-1867

From 1866 to 1868 a series of bank robberies took place in the area around Kearney. Jesse and Frank were each suspected of participating in these hold-ups, although no proof was ever found that they had.

Then on December 7, 1869, two men rode into Gallatin, Missouri and halted in front of the Daviess County Savings Bank. One man stayed outside with the horses while the other entered the bank. It was noon, and the town was quiet. Inside the bank were Captain John W. Sheets, the cashier, and his clerk. The stranger, who looked like a well-to-do cattleman, asked Sheets to change a hundred dollar bill. As Sheets was counting out the money, the second man entered the bank. He whispered a few words to his partner, then drew a Colt Navy pistol and fired twice, hitting Sheets in the head and in the chest. Sheets crumpled to the floor, dead.

The bandits took the keys to the safe and opened it, removing about seven hundred dollars. While they were occupied with the money, the clerk made a dash for safety. The bandits fired wildly, hitting him once in the arm, but the clerk managed to get outside and give the alarm. Grabbing up the money, the two outlaws ran from the bank. As they reached their horses, townspeople opened fire on them. The horses were startled by the shots. As the man who had killed Sheets tried to mount, his horse spooked. The bandit lost his balance and fell. He was dragged for about thirty feet, face down, before he could unhook his heel from the stirrup and release himself. His partner wheeled and rode back to help him onto his own horse. Then the two raced out of town, riding double.

The bandits knew that they would not be able to outdistance pursuers while both were riding the same horse. The double load would slow the animal down too much. It was a serious problem, but they were lucky. About a mile out of town they met a farmer named Daniel Smoot who happened to be riding a fine horse. Forcing Smoot to dismount, they stole his horse. After that, they were able to travel a lot faster. However, they still had a problem: they needed a guide. They seized a Methodist minister named Helm and forced him at gunpoint to take them on back roads around the next town. Before releasing him, one of the bandits told Helm that he had just shot a man named Cox, who had killed his brother, Bill Anderson, during the war. Major S. P. Cox had in fact killed Anderson, the Jameses' former guerrilla chief. Possibly the bandits mistook the cashier, Sheets, for Cox, since the two looked somewhat alike, and both lived in Gallatin. The outlaw's claim that he was Bill Anderson's brother seems to have been made simply to throw off suspicion.

The robbery had been a success, but a major clue was left in Gallatin: the skittish horse that had thrown John Sheets' murderer. An investigation soon turned up the horse's owner. On December 16 the Kansas City *Times* reported that the animal belonged to a "young man named James whose mother and stepfather live about four miles from Centreville [Kearney], Clay County." The story went on to say: "Both he and his brother are desperate men, having had much experience in horse and revolver work." The horse belonged to Jesse James.

A reward of $3000 was offered for the capture of Jesse and of Frank, believed to be the second bandit in the Gallatin hold-up. Two men from Gallatin decided to take on the job. They persuaded the deputy sheriff of Liberty, John S. Thomason, and his son, Oscar, to assist them. Together, the four men headed for the Samuel farm. They were ill-prepared for what faced them. Jesse and Frank usually kept horses saddled and ready in case they had to make a quick escape. Warned of Sheriff Thomason's approach by a young boy, they burst out of the Samuel barn at a gallop, jumped the back fence, and raced away. The posse fired after them and tried to follow, but three of their horses balked at the fence. Only Sheriff Thomason's mount went over. Unwilling to take on the two brothers by himself, Thomason dismounted in order to get off a more accurate shot. As he was firing, his horse bolted and was hit in the head by one of the Jameses. Sheriff Thomason had to walk back to the Samuel farm and borrow another horse to take him home.

After that, the James brothers went into hiding. Having lived in Kearney most of their lives, they knew the woods and back roads well. And there were many neighbors, family and friends, who were willing to shield them. Still, they were not content to remain on the defensive. Jesse decided to make a move of his own. He sent a letter to a friendly newspaper editor claiming that he was innocent of the murder and robbery in Gallatin. He said that he would have been willing to give himself up except that he knew his wartime enemies would not allow him to have a fair trial. The letter was published, along with signed statements by respected citizens vouching for Jesse's good character. The Samuels swore that Jesse was at home on the day of the hold-up and that the horse found in Gallatin had been sold to a man from Kansas two days before. Jesse's ruse worked. Tempers cooled, and little by little the accusations were forgotten. He was to use the device of letters to newspapers and sworn alibis again and again from then on.

CHAPTER FIVE

Easy Pickings

It wasn't until more than a year later that Jesse and Frank attempted another hold-up. This time their target was the town of Corydon, Iowa, just across the Missouri border. Two other ex-guerrillas went along on the raid: Clell Miller and Cole Younger. Younger had fought with Frank James under Quantrill and was suspected of participating in a string of recent robberies.

On June 3, 1871, most of Corydon's population had turned out at the Methodist church to listen to a famous speaker, Henry Clay Dean. At the Ocobock Brothers' Bank, the hold-up went according to pattern. The cashier was asked to change a hundred dollar bill. While he was getting the money, the bandits drew their pistols. Then they tied up the cashier, left him in a back room, and strolled out of the bank with roughly $10,000 stacked inside a wheat sack.

Before leaving town the gang stopped at the church. In a gesture characteristic of Jesse, one of the robbers interrupted the speech to announce that somebody had been to the bank and had tied up the cashier. He suggested that it might be a good idea to go over to the bank and see what the trouble was. It took a while for the crowd to decide whether or not to treat this remark as a joke. By the time anyone got around to checking, the gang was gone.

A posse sent out a half hour later reported having a gun battle with the outlaws but finally lost their trail.

Jesse wrote a letter to the newspapers claiming that he had nothing to do with the Corydon affair. Clell Miller was arrested near his home in Kearney and sent to Iowa to stand trial, but he was eventually released for lack of solid evidence against him.

Ten months later, on April 29, 1872, the gang struck in Columbia, Kentucky. There were five of them this time. Two waited outside the Deposit Bank, and three entered the building. The cashier, R. A. C. Martin, refused to open the safe. One of the bandits shot and killed him. Several customers were in the bank, and when the shooting started, they darted for doors and windows. The hold-up men cleaned out the cash drawer, which contained only a few hundred dollars, and left without ever opening the safe. A posse was sent out in pursuit, but the gang got away, taking a zig-zag route back to Missouri. Detectives suspected Jesse, Frank, and Cole Younger of being in on the robbery but were unable to prove it.

In September, 1872, the Kansas City Fair was in full swing. On the 26th over 10,000 people milled about the fairgrounds. Late that afternoon three men on horseback approached the main gate. One dismounted, walked up to the ticket taker, and seized the tin box in which he kept his cash receipts. There was a struggle over the box. One of the mounted men fired at the ticket taker. The shot missed him, hitting a young girl in the leg. The bandit with the money box broke away, remounted and galloped off with his companions. They were not followed. It was believed that the three men were Jesse, Frank, and either Cole Younger or one of his brothers.

The take from the robbery must have proved a disappointment to the bandits, probably less than a thousand dollars. As it happened, most of the cash from the fairgrounds had been delivered to a local bank only minutes before their arrival.

The gang's usual practice was to split up after a robbery, then drift together again months or even a year or more later, whenever they were running short of money, to plan a new raid. The number and make-up of the gang shifted from robbery to robbery depending on who was available and how many men were needed for a particular strike. During Jesse's lifetime, there were about twenty-eight men who rode with him more or less regularly.

In May, 1873, eight months after the Kansas City raid, the gang prepared to move again. Four men were to go, probably Jesse, Frank, Cole Younger and Clell Miller. Taking their time, they crossed Missouri on horseback, heading for the little town of Ste. Genevieve near the Mississippi River. There they broke up, entering town from different directions. They met again in front of the Ste. Genevieve Savings Association. Two men entered the bank, and two stayed outside to serve as lookouts. Cashier O. D. Harris opened the safe at gunpoint and delivered about $4000 in bills and heavy silver coins. The bank president's son, Firman A. Rozier, Jr., was also working in the bank that day. Rozier waited for his chance, then ran from the building shouting that a robbery was going on. The bandits fired after him but missed. Then, expecting trouble outside, they forced the cashier to walk in front of them as they entered the street. Dragging the now-familiar wheat sack behind them, they made their way to their horses. As the four gunmen were riding out of town, the man holding the wheat sack weighed down with coins accidentally dropped it. He reined in and dismounted to pick up the sack, but as he was climbing back onto his horse, the animal was startled by the clinking coins and ran off without him. At this point a farmer rode past. Waving their revolvers, the robbers ordered him to bring back the runaway horse. He did, and the gang continued out of Ste. Genevieve. There was a half-hearted pursuit, but the bandits had faded into the countryside like winter twilight.

CHAPTER SIX

Train Robbery

In 1873 the James-Younger gang seized on a new prey: the railroads. They were not the first to hold up a train. The Reno brothers had done it seven years earlier, and there had been at least twenty train robberies since. But the exploits of the Jameses and Youngers eclipsed any that had gone before.

About this time, Jesse began to emerge as the leader of the gang. In the immediate post-war years Jesse had followed his brother and Cole Younger, both older and more experienced men. The switch to a daring new form of robbery is one indication of the change. Jesse was hot-headed, impulsive, flamboyant. He is much more likely to have prompted the switch than the stolid Frank or Cole.

Another piece of evidence is a description of the band's leader, given by a farmer at whose home they ate dinner after their first train hold-up: "Five feet seven or eight inches tall, light hair, blue eyes, heavy sandy whiskers, broad shoulders, short nose, a little turned up; high, broad forehead; looked to be a well-educated man not used to work." It was a description of Jesse James. One thing the farmer got wrong was Jesse's age. He guessed thirty-six to forty. Jesse was only twenty-five years old at the time.

The Jameses had learned that a large gold shipment was being sent East by way of the Chicago, Rock Island and Pacific Railroad on July 21. Seven men rode north into Iowa to intercept the train. They picked a spot near the town of Adair where there was a sharp bend in the track, forcing trains to slow down. Just before sundown on the 21st, the seven bandits came out of the woods in which they had hidden their horses. Using a spike-bar, they loosened one of the rails. They tied a rope around the loose rail and replaced the rail in line so that it looked as it had originally. They strung the other end of the rope to a hiding place in the brush alongside the tracks. Then they settled down to wait.

The train appeared around the curve at about 8:30 that night. The bandits yanked the rope, pulling the loose rail out of place. John Rafferty, the engineer of the train, saw the rail move and threw the throttle into reverse. But it was too late to stop. The engine plunged through the break in the rails, skipped the track, and rolled over on its side. Rafferty was crushed to death inside the cab. Instead of jumping to safety, he had stayed at the controls, trying desperately to halt the train in time. As a result, although the fireman and some of the passengers were shaken up, no one else was killed.

The bandits, hoods concealing their faces, moved quickly. Two of them entered the express car, drew their guns, and forced the messenger to open the safe. To their fury, they discovered that the safe contained only two or three thousand dollars. They had stopped the wrong train. The gold shipment was to pass through safely half a day later.

The outlaws stomped through the coaches, stripping the startled passengers of money and jewelry. Then they mounted their horses and rode off into the darkness. The passengers and crew had to walk to the next town.

Railroad men soon organized to go after the outlaw band. They traced the gang back to Missouri but lost them somewhere in Jackson County. Once again Jesse and Frank had melted away into the friendly country they knew best.

❀ ❀ ❀

Late on the morning of January 15, 1874 five armed men held up the stage coach running between Malvern, Arkansas and the resort of Hot Springs. One of the bandits, probably Frank James, ordered the driver to pull up. The fourteen passengers were hustled out of the coach and searched for cash and other valuables. As the passengers emptied their pockets and hand luggage, a big, solidly-built man later identified as Cole Younger, asked one of the victims if he, or anyone else on board, was a former Confederate soldier. The passenger, George R. Crump, replied that he had been and named his company and commanding officer. In response, Younger is said to have returned Crump's watch and money, declaring that the gang never stole from Southerners, particularly not from ex-Confederate soldiers. He went on to say that he and his companions had been forced to become outlaws because they had been terrorized by Northerners after the war and denied the chance to settle down peacefully.

Cole's first statement was simply not true. This is the only known case in which the bandits refused to steal from a Southerner. In fact, many of the banks and railroads they plundered were located either in Southern states, or in states such as Missouri in which there were large numbers of Confederate sympathizers. But the incident led many people to believe that the gang's crimes were intended as a way of taking revenge against the North.

The second part of Cole's little speech had some truth to it. His own father, though loyal to the Federal government, had been robbed and murdered by Federal troops. His mother was harassed by Union men who blamed her for her son's activities as a Confederate guerrilla. The family's large farm was lost during the war. After the war, the wounds were slow to heal.

❀ ❀ ❀

Although the gang's first train robbery had been a bust, it

wasn't long before they tried again. This time they added a fresh twist.

Dark was falling as five masked men entered the ramshackle depot at Gad's Hill, a tiny, isolated station on the Iron Mountain Railroad in southeastern Missouri. It was January 31, 1874.

The bandits took over the station, holding guns on the station master and four or five townspeople in the depot. One of the masked men set a red signal on the tracks. The express from St. Louis was due to pass by at 5:40. Responding to the flag, the engineer put on the brakes. As the train slowed to a halt, the conductor hopped down to the station platform. There he faced a masked man pointing a pistol at him. The conductor was ushered into the station house with the other prisoners. The engineer and the fireman were held under guard by a second bandit. The rest of the gang boarded the train.

As they moved through the cars, the bandits studied each of the male passengers, asking their names, looking closely at their hands to see if the palms were calloused from physical work, even forcing one man to take off his clothes. They claimed that they didn't want to rob any working people but only the rich. More likely, they were trying to find out whether any of the men on board were detectives, and soft hands would have been one clue. If they had found a detective there is little question that they would have killed him on the spot.

Having finished with the passengers, the outlaws cut open the mail sacks, searching for cash and money orders. They also broke into the express safe. Their total take was well over $12,000.

Just before riding off, one of the gang handed a crew member an envelope. It contained a description of the hold-up in the form of a press release ready for printing in the newspapers. The amount of the theft had been left blank, to be filled in later. The press release was another touch characteristic of Jesse, combining bravado with a roguish sense of humor.

The statement was designed to impress. It called the robbery: "the most daring on record," and portrayed the bandits as: "all large men, none under six feet tall . . . all mounted on fine blooded horses." It closed with the line: "There is a hell of an excitement in this part of the country." The details of the robbery were described pretty much as they happened. It was a bold stroke, and one that would win the gang wide notoriety.

Long before a posse could be organized, the bandits had vanished.

CHAPTER SEVEN

Pursuit

The Adair and Gad's Hill robberies made the James brothers national figures. Detectives had been on their trail from time to time for the past six years. Now the hunt grew hotter.

The biggest and best known private detective organization in those days was the Pinkerton National Detective Agency, whose headquarters were in Chicago, Illinois. Pinkerton men had tracked the James gang on and off since the Corydon robbery in 1871. After the train hold-ups, the agency was hired by the railroad companies on a continuing basis. A special Pinkerton branch office was established in Kansas City to direct the search for the gang. The Pinkertons' efforts resulted in a series of calamities, the last of which badly damaged the agency's reputation.

Early in 1874 Pinkerton men developed a plan to capture the James brothers. The agent chosen to carry out the plan was John W. Whicher, twenty-six years old and only recently married. Whicher had worked in the Pinkertons' Chicago office, and although young, was considered one of their best men.

On March 10 Whicher arrived in Liberty, Missouri, just twelve miles from Kearney, where the Samuel farm was located. The next day he went to the Commercial Bank, deposited some money from Pinkerton funds, and asked to speak to the bank's president, D. J. Adkins. Whicher told Adkins of the scheme to bring in the Jameses. Adkins warned him that the idea was foolhardy and had little chance of working. Whicher next sought out O.P. Moss, a former county sheriff. Moss, too, advised the young Pinkerton agent against the plan, stressing that the James brothers were smart, wary, and dangerous.

But Whicher ignored the warnings. Back at his hotel he changed into the clothes of a farm hand, which were to serve as a disguise. Then he caught the late afternoon train to Kearney. The only real precaution he took was to carry a concealed pistol.

John Whicher reached Kearney just before nightfall and began the four-mile walk to the Samuel farm. His plan was simple. Simple and foolish. He intended to ask the Samuels for a job as a field hand. When he saw his chance, he would pull out his gun and take the unsuspecting James brothers prisoner.

Between two and three o'clock the following morning the ferryman at a place called Blue Mills, not far south of Kearney, was awakened by four men who asked to be taken across the Missouri river to the Jackson County side. One of the four was tied up. There was a gag in his mouth. When the ferryman asked about this, he was told that the bound man was a captured horse thief and that the other three were chasing his partners.

After sunup a man's body was found lying by the edge of a Jackson County road, several miles from the Blue Mills ferry. The dead man had been shot in the head and in the chest. The body was later identified by the initials J. W. W., which were tattooed on the right arm. It was John Whicher.

According to one story, a friend of the Jameses had spotted Whicher in Liberty and rode out to warn them before the young detective ever arrived in Kearney. It is likely that Whicher was murdered on the Jackson County side of the river in order to throw off suspicion. Frank James was apparently not among the three men who accompanied Whicher across the river but judging from the ferryman's eyewitness description, Jesse was. John

Whicher paid with his life for underestimating the James brothers. He was not the last to make the same mistake.

Less than a week later the Pinkertons launched an effort to capture Cole Younger and his brothers. Under false names, two Pinkerton agents, Louis J. Lull and John Boyle, were dispatched to Clair County in southwestern Missouri, where the Youngers had been known to hide out. There they persuaded an ex-deputy sheriff, Edwin B. Daniel, to join the search. Daniel led agents Lull and Boyle to Monegaw Springs. The three men stopped at the farm of Theodoric Snuffer, a friend of the Youngers. Boyle had met the Youngers and was afraid they would recognize him if they happened to be with Snuffer. He waited outside while Lull and Daniel went to the door on the pretext of asking directions to the house of a certain Widow Simms, who lived down the road. Snuffer told Lull and Daniel the way, and they left.

As it turned out, John and Jim Younger, two of Cole's brothers, were visiting Snuffer that day. Keeping out of sight, they listened to the conversation at the door and watched as Lull and Daniel departed. Instead of following Snuffer's directions the two men turned the opposite way. That was enough to alert the Youngers. Something was wrong. They rode out after the strangers and caught up with them a short distance from the house. By this time Boyle had rejoined his companions. The Youngers called out for the three men to stop. Boyle drew his gun, then lost his nerve and fled without firing, abandoning his two partners. The Youngers fired after him but failed to hit him. Turning to Lull and Daniel, they ordered both men to drop their guns. Jim Younger got off his horse to pick up the weapons. Then John Younger asked the two strangers who they were and what they were doing in the area.

Lull, fearing that he and Daniel would be shot whatever

answers they gave, drew a Smith and Wesson revolver that he had kept hidden in his back pocket and fired at John Younger, hitting him in the neck. Both Youngers fired back at Lull, whose startled horse sprang off the road into the brush. John Younger fired again, and Lull toppled from his mount. At the same time Daniel spurred his horse in an attempt to get away. Jim Younger fired after him and hit him in the back of the neck. The wound proved fatal.

Moments later, John Younger died of the bullet wound he had received from Lull's Smith and Wesson. He was eventually buried in Theodoric Snuffer's orchard. Lull lived for six more weeks, long enough for his family to come from Chicago to be with him. Then he, too, died from his gunshot wound.

Cole Younger was later to write of his dead brother: "Poor John! He has been hunted down and shot like a wild beast, and never was a boy more innocent. But there is a day coming when the secrets of all hearts will be open before that All-Seeing Eye, and every act of our lives will be scrutinized. Then will his skirts be white as the driven snow, while those of his accusers will be doubly dark."

Cole's biblical-sounding prose may have moved some, but he left out a few key facts. Among other things, he failed to mention that his twenty-four-year-old brother was wanted on a murder charge in Texas.

On April 24, 1874 Jesse married his cousin, Zerelda Mimms. The wedding ceremony took place near Kearney, at the home of one of Zee's sisters. The Reverend William James, Jesse and Zee's uncle, performed the service.

It had been nine years since Jesse and Zee became engaged. One reason for the long delay was opposition on both sides of the family. Zee's mother was against it. And so was Jesse's. It may also be that Jesse did not want to expose Zee to the dangers of living with a hunted man. Whatever the reasons, there came a time when the young couple decided they could wait no longer.

Jesse was to say of Zee: "We had been engaged for nine years, and through good and evil report, and not withstanding the lies that have been told upon me and the crimes laid at my door, her devotion to me never wavered for a moment." To Jesse's credit, his devotion to her seems to have been equally strong.

Several months later, Frank James also married. His new wife was Annie Ralston, the seventeen-year-old daughter of a Jackson County farmer. The couple ran off together suddenly, without telling anyone their plans. Annie's law-abiding parents were understandably shocked when they discovered whom she had married.

Marriage did not slow down the James brothers. In May, 1874 they held up a stage coach near San Antonio, Texas. One of the passengers, an Episcopal bishop named Gregg, begged the bandits not to take his watch, which had been given to him by a close friend. The bishop was told that he did not need the watch since his Master, Jesus Christ, never owned one.

On December 7, the gang raided the Tishimingo Savings Bank in Corinth, Mississippi. Later, they stopped a Kansas Pacific Railroad express train near Muncie, Kansas. They had the express car uncoupled and forced the engineer to pull it several hundred yards ahead of the rest of the train. Then they looted the detached car at their leisure.

The Pinkerton detective agency was stung by the loss of three of their men and by their failure to capture the elusive Jameses. Working in complete secrecy this time, they sent an agent named Jack Ladd to keep watch on the two brothers. Ladd went to work for Daniel Askew, who owned a farm next to the

Samuels' place. Upon arriving, Ladd circulated in the neighborhood, learning what he could and keeping an eye on the Samuel farm to find out when the Jameses came to visit their mother. At last he gave the signal that Jesse and Frank had appeared.

On the night of January 25, 1875 a specially-arranged train stopped at Kearney. A group of Pinkerton agents got off the train and made their way to the Samuel farm. In the darkness they crept up to the silent house and fanned out around it.

Suddenly, one of the Pinkerton men lit a flare made of balled cotton soaked in kerosene and hurled it through the kitchen window. Inside, the sleeping family awoke with a start. Seeing the burning flare, Dr. and Mrs. Samuel prodded at it with sticks and managed to roll it into the fireplace where it could do no harm.

Then a second flaming ball came hurtling through the window. It looked much like the first, and again the Samuels poked at it with sticks. But the sticks proved too light to budge this second fireball. Dr. Samuel grabbed a shovel and scooped it into the hearth. At that moment the flare exploded with the force of a bomb.

The result was horrible. An iron fragment hit the Samuels' son, Archie, gouging a ragged hole in his left side. The nine-year-old boy, Jesse and Frank's half-brother, died minutes later. Mrs. Samuel's right arm was badly torn. Eventually her hand had to be amputated. A young boy who worked for the Samuels was also wounded but recovered without permanent harm.

The Pinkerton men fled soon after the explosion and were picked up by the train that had brought them to Kearney. In the confusion following the blast, one of the agents dropped his gun. It was later found lying on the ground. The initials P. G. G., standing for Pinkerton's Government Guard, were clearly marked on the handle. That left no doubt in anyone's mind about who was responsible for Archie Samuel's death.

The iron ball that had caused the damage turned out not to

be a bomb, as was first thought. It was a flare filled with kerosene or some other liquid that burned easily. The ball had burst apart when exposed to the heat from the fire in the hearth. But the fact that the explosion was accidental did not prevent the Pinkertons from being severely criticized. Newspapers all over the country carried the story of the night attack. Most of them called it a cowardly and inexcusable outrage. The incident led to an outpouring of sympathy for the Jameses.

On the night of the explosion Jack Ladd disappeared from the Askew farm. He was never seen again. Then one evening two months afterward, Daniel Askew was shot and killed on his front porch as he returned home with a bucket of springwater. Neighborhood talk had connected Askew with the attack on the Samuels. No one knows for sure who shot him.

There is some evidence that either Jesse or Frank was at home during the Pinkerton raid. If so, whichever it was escaped unseen.

CHAPTER EIGHT

High Water Mark

1876 marked a major turning point for the Jameses. It was the year of one of their most dramatic and profitable hold-ups, and it was the year of their severest defeat.

The James brothers had devised a number of ways to avoid getting caught. For over ten years the law seemed powerless to stop them. No posse, no big-city detective, no reward could bring about their capture.

One practical problem in capturing the Jameses was the lack of identification. They were careful not to allow pictures of themselves to fall into unfriendly hands. Eyewitness accounts of their robberies tended to be vague or inaccurate. Without detailed descriptions, it was difficult to prove that the brothers had actually committed a particular crime. To further confuse the issue, they usually developed alibis backed up by sworn statements from friends and relatives. The result was that the Jameses could go about in public without much risk of being recognized as wanted men.

Friends also helped Jesse and Frank more directly, hiding them from pursuers or lending them fresh horses. If the Jameses happened to be in an area where they knew no one, they would simply stop at a farmhouse and ask for a meal or shelter for the night. When they left, they usually paid generously for their food and board.

Some people who might have identified the Jameses, or given information about them, failed to do so out of fear that it would put their own lives in danger. Witnesses who had recognized the Jameses or the Youngers at the scene of a robbery would suddenly change their minds and claim they weren't sure. Lawmen who traced the gang into Clay or Jackson counties often met with hostility from local residents.

In addition to fear, there was public admiration for the James gang. Although the Jameses did steal from individuals, what received the most attention in newspapers were the robberies aimed at big business: banks and railroads. And there were many who looked upon big business as the enemy. Banks loaned money, often at high rates of interest, and took over homes and farms if the loans were not repaid on time. Railroad tracks cut through valuable farmland, and the railroad companies were sometimes slow about payment for damage done to crops or livestock. Many people believed that stealing from banks and railroads was simply reclaiming money that had been sweated out of the poor.

The Jameses and Youngers shrewdly exploited every available strain of sympathy. They posed as Robin Hood figures who refused to steal from women or from the impoverished; they maintained that they would not rob former Confederates. Little by little the seeds were sown for a legend that was to turn the Jameses from ruthless brigands into heroes.

It was an atmosphere in which the gang thrived. But the James brothers were becoming victims of their own success. They had begun to grow careless.

On July 7, 1876, the Jameses and Youngers held up a train at Rocky Cut, near Otterville, in central Missouri. This robbery was different from all the others in one important way: for the first time a member of the gang was caught, confessed to the crime, and named others who had taken part in it. The man who confessed was Hobbs Kerry, who had never ridden with the Jameses before. He was not a hardened veteran like the others, and under questioning he broke down and identified his companions as the James brothers, Cole and Bob Younger, Clell Miller, Bill Stiles (who also used the name Bill Chadwell) and Samuel Wells (also known as Charlie Pitts.)

At first the robbery went smoothly. Under cover of darkness, the bandits surprised the old man who served as watchman at the Lamine River bridge. At about 10:00 P.M. a Missouri Pacific train chugged into sight. Using the watchman's red lantern, the gang signaled the engineer to stop. The outlaws wore red bandanas and masks to hide their faces. Splitting up, they took charge of the train almost as soon as it rolled to a halt. One man, probably Frank James, stayed outside, firing his Colt revolver to frighten and confuse the passengers and crew. Several others overpowered the engineer and fireman and herded them back to the baggage car where the baggagemaster, Pete Conklin, was being held prisoner by three of their partners.

The bandits demanded the key to the safe. Conklin told them that he didn't have it, the express messenger did. The bandits forced Conklin to help them find the messenger, John B. Bushnell. However, Bushnell told the outlaws that he didn't have the key, either. By this time the bandits were getting impatient. They threatened to shoot Bushnell unless he delivered the missing key. Facing the muzzle of a loaded gun, Bushnell admitted that he had slipped the key to the brakeman. The brakeman was soon found and handed over the key.

Then a new problem developed. There were two safes on board the train. The key the bandits now had fitted the U.S. Express safe. They promptly opened this safe, removed the money inside, and stuffed it into the usual wheat sack. That left the other safe, which belonged to the Adams Express Company. One of the bandits asked Bushnell where the key to this safe was. It turned out that the key was not on board. The Adams was a so-called "through" safe, which meant that it was being shipped through locked, without a key to open it.

A bandit later identified as Bob Younger found a coal pick and slammed it into the Adams safe. He swung again and again, banging away at the hinges and door. But the metal safe would not give. Then a second bandit, a big, burly bear of a man said to have been Cole Younger, took the pick, swung it over his head, and brought it crashing down on the safe. Finally the pick bit through metal, making a small hole. The big man stuck his hands in, but he had a fist "like a ham" and couldn't reach the cash inside. A slim robber wearing gloves offered to try. It was Jesse James. Jesse managed to get his hand through the opening and found a leather pouch. But the pouch was too bulky to pull through the hole. Jesse took out a knife, slashed open the pouch, and removed the money handful by handful, dumping it into the wheat sack.

There were other complications, too. While the safes were being rifled, a boy who sold newspapers on the train drew a gun and fired at one of the bandits. He missed, and the weapon was quickly taken away from him. One of the passengers, a woman, also had a pistol. She refused to give it to a male passenger who asked for the use of it and threatened to shoot anyone who tried to rob her.

Other passengers, thrown into a near-panic by the gunshots and loud yells they could hear outside, frantically hid their cash and watches. They stowed their valuables everywhere: under seats, in air ducts, in a coal box, even in their socks. Some passengers crouched under their seats to keep out of sight. As Jesse was passing through a coach, he tripped over the feet of a tall man whose legs stuck out from under the seat where he was cowering in fright. The man pleaded for his life, certain that he was about to be shot. But Jesse simply laughed and continued on through the car.

Among those on the train was a minister from Bedford, New York. During the robbery he prayed out loud and sang hymns to keep up the passengers' spirits.

After cleaning out the two safes, the bandits mounted their horses and rode off. The conductor wired news of the hold-up from the town of Tipton, but an effort to follow the gang came to nothing. The bandits had escaped with about $17,000.

Investigations by the St. Louis police department led straight to Hobbs Kerry. Kerry, who had been talking too freely and flashing fat stacks of bills, was identified as one of the strangers seen near Otterville just before the hold-up. Under pressure he broke down and confessed. Having named the others in the robbery, he was let off with a two-year jail sentence.

Jesse wrote two letters to the Kansas City *Times* claiming that Kerry's confession was false. His tone was a blend of arrogance and injured innocence. He wrote: "You have published Hobbs Kerry's confession, which makes it appear that the Jameses and the Youngers were the Rocky Cut robbers. If there was only one side to be told, it would probably be believed by a good many people that Kerry told the truth. But his so-called confession is a well-built pack of lies from beginning to end. I never heard of Hobbs Kerry, Charlie Pitts, or William Chadwell until Kerry's arrest. I can prove my innocence by eight good, well-known men of Jackson County, and show conclusively that I was not at the train robbery. . . . Kerry knows that the Jameses and Youngers can't be taken alive, and that is why he has put it on us."

There were probably some who believed this. Others simply admired the daring of the flat denial. But now, for the first time, names had been named by an insider, and Jesse's pose of blamelessness was wearing thin.

Next time there were to be more than names to leave a record behind. Next time there were to be stiff bodies in the streets.

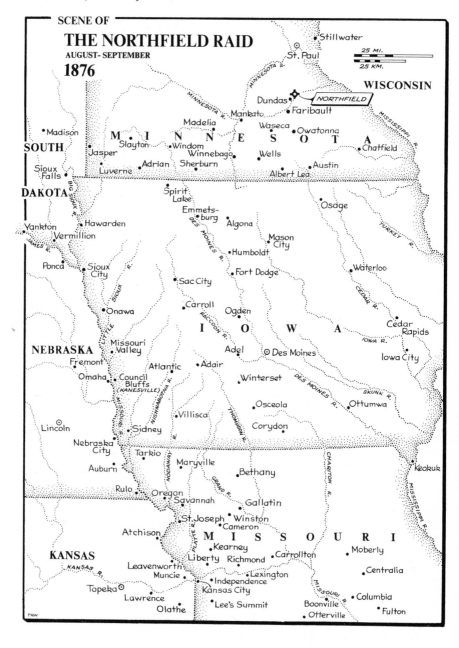

SCENE OF

THE NORTHFIELD RAID
AUGUST- SEPTEMBER
1876

CHAPTER NINE

The Northfield Raid

Just two months after the Otterville hold-up the gang struck again. They had learned from the experience with Hobbs Kerry, and this time each man was a tested veteran. There were eight of them: Jesse and Frank, Cole, Jim, and Bob Younger, Clell Miller, Samuel Wells, and Bill Stiles.

Since Missouri lawmen were on the alert for them, the gang decided to stake out fresh territory to the north—Minnesota. The key to the plan was Bill Stiles. Stiles had lived in Minnesota and knew his way around. The others were counting on him to serve as guide in this unfamiliar country.

Travelling in groups of two and three, the gang crossed the Minnesota border in mid-August. As usual, they rode sleek, fast horses. Jesse himself often raced his horses at county fairs, taking first prize money more than once. He knew horses, and he was an expert rider, as were his companions. On the journey to Minnesota the men wore long, floppy linen dusters of the kind used by cattlemen to protect their clothes from the dust of the roads on cattle drives. The outfits served two purposes. First, they acted as a disguise, since passersby assumed the men who wore them were cattle buyers. Second, the dusters helped hide the small armory of weapons each gang member had with him. Jesse, for example, sometimes carried as many as six guns.

The gang took their time, scouting southern Minnesota carefully. They stopped in a number of towns to look over banks that promised to be easy marks. They studied escape routes, watching for bottlenecks where they could be trapped and for timber where they could hide. At night they stayed at hotels and farmhouses, paying for their rooms and meals like ordinary businessmen. Whenever possible, they engaged local citizens in conversation, hoping to pick up scraps of information that would help them choose a target.

There was one false start. Jesse and four other gang members spent a weekend in the town of Mankato, which seemed to meet all their requirements. But as they were looking the town over, they ran into a man who recognized Jesse and notified the police. The five bandits continued to behave like businessmen, and although they were watched, no move was made against them.

On Monday morning, as Jesse and his companions rode past the bank, they noticed a crowd looking at some construction work that was going on next door. Heads turned as they went by. The bandits returned later that day to find a crowd still gathered by the bank and still curious about the five strangers. It was enough to make the outlaws skittish. They decided to leave Mankato.

The gang drifted on to the northeast, heading for the little town of Northfield, set in a belt of prosperous farm country. It was one of the places they had scouted earlier. The outlaws met in a patch of woods several miles outside of town. Then, their plans made, they split into three bands and started toward Northfield.

Early on the afternoon of September 7, 1876, Bob Younger, Sam Wells and Jesse James crossed the wooden bridge over the Cannon River, which ran through Northfield. They were facing east, toward Bridge Square. To their right, at the far end of the square, was the two-story stone building called the Scriver Block. Around the corner, on the Division Street side of the Scriver Block, was the entrance to the First National Bank of Northfield.

The three men tied their horses at the front of the bank and sat down on some wooden boxes as though they were just passing time. Shortly afterwards, two more men turned the corner onto Division Street. They were Cole Younger and Clell Miller. Bob Younger, Sam Wells and Jesse rose to their feet and strolled into the bank, leaving the door open. Clell Miller dismounted, walked to the front of the bank and closed the door behind them. Then he began pacing slowly up and down in front of the bank's entrance. Cole Younger got off his horse in the middle of the street and worked at tightening his saddle strap. From where he stood he could see what was happening along the entire length of the street in both directions.

So far everything had gone according to plan.

Then, suddenly, it all began to come apart. A local hardware store owner, J. S. Allen, had noticed the five strangers in town. There was something about them that he didn't like. He approached the bank entrance, where he was stopped by Clell Miller. Miller told him to get away from the door. Convinced, now, that something was wrong, Allen scurried around the corner to Bridge Square shouting: "Get your guns, boys! Get your guns! They're robbing the bank!"

Henry Wheeler, a twenty-two-year-old medical student, had been sitting in front of his father's drugstore on Division Street when the bandits entered town. Curious, he got up and moved to a point from which he could watch the bank entrance. Now he, too, joined in shouting the alarm.

Cole Younger and Clell Miller re-mounted their horses. Cole told Wheeler to get off the street. Then he and Miller rode back and forth, firing shots over their heads and ordering other passersby to get inside. One man who failed to move was shot and killed. He was a Swedish immigrant named Nicholas Gustavson who did not speak English.

The next few minutes were chaotic. Frank James and Bill Stiles, who were stationed in Bridge Square, guarding the escape route, heard the unexpected noise and started across the square.

Henry Wheeler, the young medical student, rushed into the Dampier Hotel on Bridge Square looking for a weapon. He found an old Civil War rifle but could only collect three cartridges for it. Wheeler then took up a position at a second floor window and waited for the chance to get off a good shot.

By this time, J. S. Allen had returned to his hardware store and was handing out loaded guns. One man who accepted a shotgun from Allen was Elias Stacy. Stacy entered Division Street on the run, aimed the shotgun and fired. He hit Clell Miller in the face and neck with birdshot, knocking him off his horse. But Miller managed to remount and retreated to a safer position.

Meanwhile, Anselm Manning, who owned a hardware store near Allen's, grabbed a rifle from his store window and dashed out into the street. Unable to get off a clean shot at any of the bandits, Manning fired at the only target he had, one of the gang's horses. His bullet brought down Bob Younger's mount. Manning's next shot hit Cole Younger in the leg. Manning reloaded, then spotted Bill Stiles, sitting on his motionless horse some distance away. Taking careful aim, he fired. Stiles tumbled from his horse. The bullet had struck him in the chest. He was dead.

From the second-floor window of the Dampier Hotel, Henry Wheeler fired at Jim Younger, missing him. Younger looked up but could not tell where the shot had come from. Wheeler had only two bullets left. He sighted his carbine on Clell Miller. When he had Miller lined up precisely, he gently squeezed the trigger. The bullet hit Miller in the right shoulder and opened an artery. The bandit plunged to the ground, where he lay bleeding to death.

Inside the bank there was more trouble. The regular cashier happened to be out of town. His place had been taken by Joseph L. Heywood, a bookkeeper. There were two other employees in the bank: the teller, A. E. Bunker, and Frank Wilcox, Heywood's assistant. The three bandits—Bob Younger, Sam Wells, and Jesse—vaulted over the counter with guns drawn. They demanded to know which of the startled bank workers was the cashier. Each in turn denied that he was. Settling on Heywood, who was in the cashier's seat, the bandits ordered him to open the safe. Heywood replied that the safe operated on a time lock and that he could not open it until the hour for which the lock had been set.

The door of the vault where the safe was kept stood open. Sam Wells moved toward it to investigate. Coming from behind his desk, Joseph Heywood rushed over and tried to slam the vault door shut, trapping Wells inside. Jesse grabbed Heywood and pulled him away before he could close the door. Insisting that Heywood open the safe, Jesse threatened him with a knife, then slashed the blade across his throat. Heywood managed to break away, shouting: "Murder! Murder!" Moving fast, Jesse caught up with him and knocked him down with a blow from his pistol. Again he demanded that Heywood open the safe. Again Heywood refused. Then Sam Wells bent low and fired a shot near where Heywood lay, trying to scare him.

At this point the teller, Bunker, darted through a back room from which there was a door to the street. The door was closed, and blinds were drawn across it. Sam Wells fired at Bunker but hit the blinds instead. Bunker plunged through the blinds, got the door open, and stumbled down the back steps. Behind him, Wells fired again, hitting him in the shoulder, but Bunker was able to get away.

The men inside the bank could hear the sounds of the gun battle raging in the street. One of the bandits posted outside called in to them: "The game's up. We're beaten."

Wells, Bob Younger, and Jesse leaped over the counter to make their escape. As the other two left the bank, Jesse turned and fired at Heywood. He missed. Heywood dragged himself to his desk and slumped down behind it. Jesse fired again. This time the bullet hit Heywood in the head. The bookkeeper sank to the floor, dead.

Outside, the three bandits faced a small, bloody war. Northfield men were firing from both sides of Division Street. Some of those who did not have guns were hurling rocks. Glass from shattered windows crashed down on the street.

Henry Wheeler, still at his post in the Dampier, had accidentally dropped his last cartridge, spilling the gunpowder. A hotel clerk had found more ammunition and rushed upstairs with it. Wheeler could see Anselm Manning and Bob Younger dodging in and out behind buildings, each trying to get a clear shot at the other. Wheeler fired, hitting Younger in the right elbow and forcing him to shift his revolver to his left hand.

By this time the six remaining bandits were thinking only about escape. Bob Younger's horse was dead. Clell Miller's and Bill Stiles' horses had run off when the two outlaws were killed. The rest of the band mounted the five horses that were left, and Cole Younger hoisted his brother, Bob, up behind him. Then the dazed and battered outlaws galloped out of town. As they rode off, Northfield's churchbells rang. The bells were an alarm signal, but they also carried the sound of victory.

The bandits, confronted with organized and persistent opposition for the first time, came away with only a few dollars in change and bills from a box on the bank counter. The safe door, which Joseph Heywood had bravely insisted was locked, had not been locked at all. A turn of the handle would have opened it.

CHAPTER TEN

Manhunt

The outlaws had escaped from Northfield, but the price was steep. Two men had been lost, one of them Bill Stiles, their intended guide. Bob Younger's right arm hung limp and clotted with blood. Jim Younger, Cole Younger, and Frank James had all been wounded. And the six survivors had only five horses. Even the weather turned against them. It began raining on the night after the robbery, and a bleak drizzle continued on and off for almost two weeks.

The bandits headed west but finding their planned route blocked, swung south on the road leading to the town of Dundas. Two men from Northfield pursued them on the horses that had belonged to Bill Stiles and Clell Miller. They soon closed on the six fugitives, but since they were so badly outnumbered, decided to pull up and wait for help.

News of the Northfield raid was telegraphed ahead, together with descriptions of the gang members. Before long, posses were assembling all along the outlaws' line of retreat.

The bandits' first problem was to find a horse for Bob Younger, who was riding double with Cole, slowing their pace. They stole a horse from a farmer's team, and Bob, having no saddle, rode bareback. When they came to a farmhouse, they managed to obtain a saddle for Bob. They told the farmer that they were lawmen chasing horse thieves and that one of their men had not had time to saddle his horse before setting out.

The band thundered on through Dundas, then turned west again. Suddenly Bob Younger's horse lost its footing and went down. The saddle strap broke, and Bob toppled to the ground, jamming his already-painful right arm. Once again he had to ride double.

The gang stole another mount from a roadside farm, but this horse lagged behind and would not keep up with the others. There was no choice but to abandon the animal. For the third time that day Bob Younger climbed up behind one of his companions. Again the bandits were forced to halt further on to pick up a new horse and saddle.

In the town of Shieldsville, the outlaws stopped to water their hard-driven horses. While the animals were drinking, the bandits noticed a pile of guns outside a small hotel. A hastily-organized posse from the town of Faribault was inside eating. The men had thoughtlessly left their arms by the door when they went in for their meal. The fugitives fired a few shots and rode off. The posse from Faribault had narrowly missed their chance to capture the James gang.

The outlaws had two or three more brushes with posses that day. Once the group from Faribault got close enough to fire at them, but no one was hit.

As word spread that six members of the James gang, large rewards on their heads, were in the area, volunteers streamed in to join the hunt. Some were ordinary citizens. Some were police or Pinkerton agents. They came by train, by horseback, and on foot. By the end of the day, two hundred men had turned out.

Since the roads were becoming dangerous, the outlaw band headed across country, hoping to lose their pursuers as they had in the past. The area they entered was a wilderness of swamp and heavy timber called the Big Woods.

The gang was moving southwest, toward Missouri. The tracking parties formed a line on the far side of the Big Woods. Gradually, the line was staked out across every possible escape route for almost fifty miles on either side of the outlaws' path. Reserve forces were sent into the woods to drive the fugitives toward the defense line, where they could be surrounded and taken prisoner.

The Jameses and Youngers spent a miserable night in the swampy forest. The rain had started, and what dry ground there was soon turned to mud. Men and horses were drenched. Worst of all, they were still less than twenty miles from Northfield.

Next day the gang broke through the make-shift defense line with surprisingly little trouble. Three men posted at a crossing of the Little Cannon River fired at them, so they fled back into the woods. Shortly afterwards they sent out a scout who found the ford unguarded. They then crossed the river and continued on to the southwest.

Realizing that the outlaws had slipped through their line, the trackers shifted further to the south and west, pushing their men fast through the dripping thickets and shuttling fresh recruits by special train to strengthen the new line.

There were now close to five hundred men in the field. Over the next two weeks five hundred more joined the hunt.

The outlaws badly needed fresh horses. They stole two mounts from a farmer, leaving two of their spent horses behind. Later, they found another horse in a field and made one more switch.

That night they camped in the rain again, spreading their saddle blankets over some bushes to shield themselves from the downpour. Bob Younger's untreated wound throbbed with infection.

The bandits' weary horses were of less and less use as what solid ground there was turned to quagmire. They decided to abandon the animals and continue on foot. Not until several days later did a posse find one of the horses tied to a tree where the outlaws had left it. The other animals had been released or had chewed through their reins and wandered off in search of forage. Word was immediately dispatched that the fugitives were on foot.

The six bandits slogged on through the swamp. If they were spotted now they had no sure means of escape. Finding a patch of high ground drier than the area around it, they decided to rest for the remainder of the day and move out again under cover of darkness. There was little to eat, and the men were hungry and wet and near exhaustion. Cole Younger and Frank James, both hit in the leg at Northfield, were limping badly.

Two days later, traveling at night and sleeping by day, the outlaws stumbled onto an empty farmhouse. They spent the next two nights there, resting from their forced march. It had now been five days since they left Northfield. They had covered less than fifty miles.

At about this time the bandits split up. It was not at all unusual for the gang to separate after a robbery in order to confuse and divide pursuers. But there may have been another reason for this particular decision. Bob Younger was badly hurt and could not travel fast. He was slowing down the others. Some say that Jesse and Frank wanted to abandon Bob so that the rest could get away. According to this story, Cole and Jim Younger angrily refused. Whatever the reason, Jesse and Frank took off by themselves, leaving the three Younger brothers and Sam Wells to manage on their own.

That night a young man named Richard Roberts, who was guarding a point on the defense line, saw two men riding double. Roberts called out for them to halt. When they tried to get away, he fired at them. The horse bolted, and both men were pitched to the ground. They scrambled to their feet and escaped, but one of them lost his hat. Roberts went over to pick it up. There was a bullet hole in it.

The young sentry had not been able to get a good look at the men's faces in the darkness, but he reported that one of them had a bandaged leg. It is likely that the two were Frank and Jesse.

The Jameses' luck began to improve after that. They stole a pair of gray horses from a farm and headed west out of Minnesota, riding bareback. Along the way they managed to pick up two saddles by posing as posse members trailing the James gang and claiming that their own saddles had been stolen. Jesse must have enjoyed that little deception. One of his favorite ploys was to ask strangers what they thought of Jesse James and whether they figured he would ever be captured.

Ten days after leaving Northfield the Jameses crossed the Minnesota state line. That night, as they rode south toward Missouri and home, they decided to trade their tired grays for two black horses they found in a field. But the blacks soon began to falter and trip. Jesse and Frank couldn't understand what was wrong. When daylight came, they examined the animals more closely. It turned out that one was totally blind, and the other had only a single good eye. It was a last comic touch to their flight.

Later that day the brothers stole a second pair of grays and moved on through South Dakota to Iowa and then into Nebraska. They bought fresh clothes, found a doctor to treat Frank's leg wound, and felt sufficiently safe to stop at farmhouses for their meals. They were near home now and out of danger.

It was a different story for the four men left behind in Minnesota. They were on foot, and Cole Younger, who was having trouble walking because of his leg injury, had to use a stick to support himself. Bob Younger's arm was swollen and discolored.

On the morning of September 21, the four fugitives passed a farm near the town of Madelia, where Cole and Sam Wells had stayed overnight on their way to Northfield, two weeks before.

The farmer's seventeen-year-old son, Oscar Suborn, took a long look at the bedraggled men as they went by. Then he told his father that he thought the strangers were part of the Northfield gang. The boy's father didn't believe him. The outlaws were supposed to have left the state long before. Thinking Oscar was imagining things, he told him to get back to his milking chores. But the boy was not about to give up so easily. When he had finished his work, he went back to the farmhouse. There he learned from his mother that the strangers had stopped to try to buy food, saying that they were on a hunting trip. Over his father's objections, Oscar decided to ride into Madelia to alert the authorities. He told his story to Colonel Thomas Vought, a Civil War veteran and owner of the Flanders House Hotel, where Cole and Sam Wells had stayed the night. Vought took the report seriously, organizing a search party that included James Glispin, the county sheriff, and several Madelia townspeople.

The posse located the ragged little band of outlaws in a swampy thicket called Hanska Slough. Sheriff Glispin called for them to halt. Instead, the fugitives pushed ahead faster. The men from Madelia fired after them, but the outlaws ducked behind a hill, then plunged on across a shallow lake, holding their guns high to keep them from getting wet.

The posse's horses balked at the edge of the water and refused to enter it. Forced to ride around the lake, the Madelia men spotted the outlaws again on the far side. A posse member named Overholt fired a shot at them. The bullet hit the stick Cole Younger had been using to prop himself up, sending it spinning out of his grip.

The outlaws were heading for a field in which a number of horses stood grazing. The sheriff and his men managed to get around in front of them, blocking the way to the horses. Shots were exchanged, and one bullet grazed Sheriff Glispin's mount.

The bandits turned and limped along the edge of a river. On the opposite side was a farmhouse. Nearby, a farmer was standing beside a team of horses. The outlaws called out to him, asking to borrow the horses so that they could pursue the Northfield gang. Unconvinced, the farmer promptly climbed up behind his team and drove it away.

Again the outlaws were cut off. Without horses, there was no way to avoid capture. Growing desperate now, they continued along the riverbank, the posse close behind them.

Then they saw another chance. Crossing the river, they came to a place where two men had camped to do some hunting. Not far away were two teams of horses. Cole and the others broke into a run. Those four horses were a ticket home. But the hunters had seen them coming and brought up their shotguns. It was too big a risk. The outlaws wheeled and started back toward the river.

The long, deadly hunt was closing. Limping ahead, the outlaws found themselves in a heavily overgrown pocket of land bordered on one side by a ridge and on the other by the river.

The posse's numbers had swelled with fresh volunteers. As the news spread that four of the Northfield gang had been cornered, more and more men rode out to be in on the finish. Trackers were sent along both banks of the river. Marksmen took up position high on the ridge, which extended in a half-circle around the flats where the outlaws had hidden. Every possible escape route was barred. The bandits were trapped and sealed in.

The next step was to flush the fugitives out from among the heavy brush. Only seven men volunteered for this operation, among them Sheriff Glispin and Colonel Vought. The seven formed a line four paces apart. Their plan was simply to rush forward toward the spot where they believed the outlaws were hidden. It was much the same technique as hunters use to flush game birds from a field. As soon as the stalkers could see their prey, they were to open fire.

At the order: "Forward!" Glispin and his men moved together at a trot. They covered twenty paces. Then thirty. And forty. At seventy paces there was still no sign of the bandits. The trackers moved on. Eighty paces. Ninety. Then Glispin's men spotted the outlaws huddled behind a clump of bushes. One of the bandits fired. The seven trackers fired back in unison, still moving forward. The outlaws returned the fire. When the posse's line was only thirty feet from where the outlaws lay, the steady, murderous barrage of gunfire ceased. In the sudden quiet it was all over.

A call went out for the fugitives to surrender. Only one of them was able to stand up. It was Bob Younger, his injured right arm in a sling. The others lay on the ground, two of them twitching in pain.

Several shots rang out from the ridge. The men stationed there had seen Bob Younger rise and failed to realize that he was surrendering. One of the bullets grazed the outlaw. Someone called out for the men on the ridge to hold their fire. Again silence filled the muddy little draw.

The bandits had been cut up horribly. Blood soaked through their torn clothes in big dark patches. The husky, bull-like Cole Younger was alive, but there were eleven bullet holes in him, including his Northfield wounds. Jim Younger had been hit five times. One bullet had smashed his jaw. Bob Younger had a fresh chest wound. Sam Wells lay crumpled and unmoving. He had been hit five times. He was dead. Miraculously, none of the trackers had been injured.

The prisoners were taken by wagon to Madelia where they were given clean clothes and a hot meal. Their wounds were tended by doctors. The outlaws were surprised at this treatment; they had expected a lynch mob. Crowds of citizens came to the jail to stare at the famous gunmen, but the mood of the onlookers seemed curious rather than hostile.

The three Younger brothers stood trial for their part in the robbery of the First National Bank and the murders of Joseph Lee

Heywood and Nicholas Gustavson. They pleaded guilty and were sentenced to life imprisonment.

The old James-Younger gang was finished. Jesse and Frank were to find others to take the places of those who were now in prison or dead, but it was never to be the same again.

CHAPTER ELEVEN

The Circle Closes

Immediately following the Northfield robbery, accounts of Jesse James' life peter out like a cold trail. For three years he and Frank went underground, leading quiet, ordinary lives under false names.

In selecting a safe place to live, the James brothers had decided on Tennessee, where they were not well known. In the fall of 1875, Jesse and Zee had moved into a farmhouse near Nashville. Zee was pregnant. Her first child, Jesse Edwards James, was born in December, 1875. To avoid causing suspicion among his new neighbors, Jesse took the name J. D. Howard. After Northfield, he settled down on the farm. He planted. He raised cattle. He raced his fine horses at local fairs. In general, he and his family seem to have been easily accepted by the community. The single dark spot in the Jameses lives during this period was the death of their infant twins. Jesse himself carved two small headstones for their graves.

Frank and Anne James rented a farm nearby, using the name Woodson. They, too, led normal lives for a time. Frank did a little farming and worked for a local lumber company. Like his brother, he occasionally raced his horses at country tracks. A son, Robert Franklin James, was born to the couple. At first he was dressed as a girl and called Mary so that if Frank were traced to Tennessee, his son could not be used as a means of identifying him. Jesse's son was also given various false names. In fact, the boy did not learn his real name or his father's until after Jesse was dead.

Jesse was not a successful farmer, and after two years the family pulled up stakes and moved on again, joining Frank and Anne on their farm. It was there that Jesse's daughter, Mary, was born in 1879.

The two James brothers were of very different natures. Frank, jug-eared and square-jawed, looked more like a judge or a prosperous banker than he did like an outlaw. A big, placid man, he had developed a taste for literature and could quote easily from Shakespeare and from the Bible. He hated the life of a fugitive. For him, the quiet years with his family on the Tennessee farm were among the happiest of his life.

Jesse—slight, sharp-featured, mercurial, was the physical and temperamental opposite of his brother. He was far too restless for a life of routine and order, and the economics of farming soon defeated him.

Before long, Jesse began to think about getting together another gang.

The public explosion came in early October of 1879 when a Chicago and Alton express train was held up at the little town of Glendale, Missouri, just twenty miles from Kansas City and right in the heart of the old James country. The robbery followed the now-familiar pattern, down to the wheat sack used to collect between five and ten thousand dollars from the express safe. The big difference was in the make-up of the gang. Jesse led the raid, but Frank, still reluctant to leave the farm, did not go along. The others were Clell Miller's brother, Ed; Wood Hite, Jesse and Frank's cousin; Bill Ryan, a heavy drinker; Dick Liddil, a hothead who was also unreliable; and a half-bright farmer named Tucker Bassham. It was a rag-tag bunch.

The hold-up itself went off smoothly, until the express agent tried to escape with the contents of the safe. He was beaten unconscious. Afterwards, Tucker Bassham began to brag openly that he was a member of the James gang. When people seemed slow to believe that, he pulled out a fat roll of bills to back up his boast.

In July, 1880 Bassham was arrested. He promptly confessed to his part in the Glendale robbery and was sent to prison. A few months later, a man who called himself Tom Hill was arrested for causing a drunken disturbance in a Tennessee barroom. He was carrying over a thousand dollars in cash in his vest, which caused suspicion. It turned out that Hill was really Bill Ryan. Tucker Bassham was granted a pardon in exchange for testifying against Ryan at his trial. It was a case of trading a little fish for a bigger fish.

The trial took place in Jackson County, where the Jameses had many relatives and friends. It was widely believed that no Jackson County jury would convict a member of the gang. But in the face of threats on his life, a courageous young prosecutor named William H. Wallace pursued the case vigorously, building up evidence and gathering witnesses prepared to testify. The jury brought back a verdict of guilty.

Times had changed. The James gang could no longer count on either sympathy or intimidation to suppress evidence of guilt. Now newspapers clamored for their arrest. Now Missourians were willing to stand up against them in the courts. Their reign of terror was coming to a close.

Then, on July 15, 1881, the gang struck again, like a dying scorpion thrashing its murderous tail. This time Frank was with them. Jesse's persuasion had finally worked.

That evening a few of the bandits slipped aboard a Chicago, Rock Island and Pacific train. Just after nightfall, as the train passed a point near Winston, Missouri, a bearded man wearing a straw hat rose from his seat in the smoking car and fired two shots at conductor William Westfall. Westfall staggered to the rear platform, then fell dead, plunging to the ground. More shots whined through the car. One of them hit and killed a passenger named Frank McMillan.

The bandits then moved to the express car. They overpowered the agent and opened the safe with his key. The contents were disappointingly meager. In frustration, one of the gang beat the agent over the head with a revolver. Other gang members stopped the train, and the men on board climbed off and made their getaway.

The cold-blooded killing of Westfall, who had put up no resistance to the robbery, is attributed to the gang's belief that he was the conductor on the special train that had brought the Pinkerton agents to Kearney on the night of the explosion at the Samuel farmhouse.

The Winston hold-up had one significant result. The newly-elected governor of Missouri, Thomas T. Crittenden, had pledged to rid the state of the outlaw bands that had preyed on it for so many years. Now Crittenden met with representatives of railroad and express companies to deliver on his promise. Less than two weeks after the Winston robbery, he made his announcement. The companies had agreed to put up five thousand dollars for the capture of either Jesse or Frank. Five thousand more would be paid for their convictions in the Glendale or Winston robberies, or on various murder charges that stood against them. And five thousand dollars was offered for the arrest and conviction of other gang members. It added up to a tempting sum.

Jack Foote was the engineer of a Chicago and Alton train heading west toward Kansas City on September 7, 1881. At nine o'clock that evening the train pulled within sight of a deep ravine called Blue Cut, just a few miles from the spot where the Glendale train had been held up two years earlier.

Ahead on the track Engineer Foote spotted a pile of stones as high as a man's chest. On top was a red signal flag attached to a stick. As Foote stopped the train, four masked men stepped up beside the cab. The leader told Foote to get the heavy pick used for coal. Other gang members rounded up the conductor and the brakeman. At first, Foote refused, but he soon realized he would be shot if he did not cooperate.

The bandits forced Foote and the fireman, John Steading, to walk back to the express car. There Foote was ordered to break down the door with the coal pick. Foote did as he was told.

Sensing that something was wrong when the train made its unscheduled stop, the express messenger, H. A. Fox, had slipped away to hide beside the tracks. The masked men commanded Foote to call him back. When Fox returned, they had him open the safe and place its contents in a sack. The bandits were furious when they saw how little the safe contained. Apparently they had planned to rob a train carrying a $100,000 shipment that was to pass through Blue Cut later the same night. They beat Fox on the head with the butt-ends of their Navy pistols until he collapsed on the floor of the car, his head bleeding.

The bandits then herded Foote and Steading toward the passenger coaches. They swaggered through the coaches roughly grabbing cash and jewelry from the frightened passengers. The leader, a tall man, his face hidden by a white cloth in which eyeholes had been cut, barked out threats. Claiming that he was Jesse James, he waved his loaded pistol and warned that this was the gun with which he had shot Conductor Westfall at Winston. What seemed to anger him the most was the announcement of the rewards. He said that the next time a reward was offered, he'd burn the entire train.

At one point during the robbery, a freight train came up

behind the halted Chicago and Alton cars. Hearing the freight's whistle, the brakeman, Frank Burton, dashed back along the tracks to flag down the approaching train before it slammed into the rear of the passenger train. The outlaws, thinking Burton was making his escape, fired after him, but he was able to stop the freight in time.

After stripping the passengers of their valuables, the bandits marched the captive trainmen back to the engine. The leader told Foote to get up into the cab, saying that he and his men would move the pile of stones blocking the tracks. It was an odd bit of courtesy.

Then he did an even more surprising thing. Remarking that he admired Foote for his bravery, he handed the engineer two silver dollars and told him to use the money to drink to Jesse James. Foote, anxious to get rid of the outlaws, said that the train crew would remove the stones themselves. With that, the bandits mounted the embankment alongside the tracks and disappeared.

There was one new member in the gang at Blue Cut. His name was Charles Ford.

CHAPTER TWELVE

Jesse James Is Dead

In the fall of 1881, Jesse and his wife and two children moved from Kansas City, where they had lived since spring, to St. Joseph, Missouri. Jesse, using the name Thomas Howard, rented a house at 1381 Lafayette Street. The house was white, with green shutters. It stood on a hill, giving it a view over most of the city, but the view wasn't what interested Jesse. He was interested in seeing anyone who approached the house a long way off. To the rear was a stable where he kept two saddled horses.

It was a bad time for Jesse. The reward money hung over his head like a noose, and the gang was dissolving around him. He was jumpy and quick to anger. Ed Miller was dead, and there were stories that Jesse himself had killed Miller because he talked too much. Clarence Hite, Jesse's cousin, pleaded guilty to taking part in the Winston robbery, and received a prison sentence of twenty-five years. His brother, Wood Hite, had been killed by Dick Liddil in a quarrel over Charles Ford's sister. Liddil buried Hite's body at night, wrapped in a horse blanket. After that, he lived in fear of Jesse's vengeance. When the pressure became too great, he surrendered to Clay County Sheriff James H. Timberlake and agreed to give evidence against his former comrades.

The gang was turning in on itself now, but it remained for Charles and Robert Ford to work the final piece of treachery. Twenty-four-year-old Charles Ford had joined the gang in time for the Blue Cut hold-up. Later, he brought his twenty-year-old brother, Robert, into the gang. Robert had been in touch with Governor Crittenden, Sheriff Timberlake, and Kansas City Police Commissioner Henry H. Craig and had made a deal with them. The details are not known, but it is clear that he was promised a reward for cutting short Jesse James' career.

By early April, 1882, the trap was baited and set. Charles and Robert Ford were staying with Jesse and his family at the house on the St. Joseph hilltop. They were planning a bank robbery in Platte City on April 4.

On April 3, the day before the intended hold-up, it was sunny and warm. After breakfast Jesse and Charles Ford went out to the stable to curry the horses. Returning to the house, they joined Bob Ford in the living room. Jesse complained of the heat and took off his coat. Worrying that some passerby would see his weapons, he unslung his gunbelt, containing two pistols, a Colt and a Smith and Wesson, both .44s. Then he picked up a dusting brush and, turning his back to the Fords, climbed onto a chair to dust a picture hanging on the wall.

Seeing the opportunity for which he had been waiting, Bob Ford drew his revolver. The hammer cocked with a snap in the quiet room. Jesse half-turned his head. The bullet from Bob Ford's gun tore through his forehead into his brain, coming out at the base of his skull. His body swung backward off the chair and hit the floor. Jesse James was dead.

Hearing the shot, Zee James dashed into the room from the kitchen. She saw Bob Ford with his gun drawn and screamed at him, calling him a murderer. Then, in an agony of grief, she went to her husband and took his bleeding head in her hands. The Fords ran from the house to notify the governor and the police that Jesse was dead.

The news spread. Before long curiosity-seekers swarmed up the hill to the little white house. At first there was uncertainty that the dead man was indeed Jesse. He had defied capture and death for so many years that it was difficult for some to imagine that he could be killed. One of those who identified the corpse was Mrs. Samuel. When asked if this were her son she cried out: "Would to God that it was not."

It was Jesse all right. The restless, pale eyes were closed, but the narrow lips, the sharply-tilted nose, the pallid skin, the light-colored beard left no room for doubt. Then, too, the old bullet wounds were plainly visible on his chest. And there was the telltale missing finger tip.

Next day the newspapers were full of the story. JESSE, BY JEHOVAH blazed the headline in the St. Joseph *Gazette*.

Jesse's body was taken by special train to Kearney for the funeral. Accompanying it were his wife, his mother, and his two children—Jesse Jr., now six, and Mary, aged three. He was buried at the Samuel farm under a large, old coffee bean tree.

The Ford brothers confessed to the murder and were sentenced to be hung. That same day Governor Crittenden issued them a pardon. Undoubtedly they received part of the reward money; how much is not known.

Bob Ford expected to be treated as a hero for killing Jesse. Instead, he has come down through history in the words of Billy Gashade's song as: "that dirty little coward that shot Mr. Howard [and] laid Jesse James in his grave."

Several years after Jesse's death, Charles Ford shot and killed himself. Bob Ford died in a Creede, Colorado barroom in 1892, when a man named Kelly emptied both barrels of a shotgun into his throat.

CHAPTER THIRTEEN

Aftermath

For six months after Jesse's death Frank James remained in hiding. But the strain of being hunted for so many years had taken its toll. On October 5, 1882 Frank James "came in". Unbuckling his gunbelt, he gave it to Governor Crittenden, saying: "I want to hand over to you that which no living man except myself has been permitted to touch since 1861, and to say that I am your prisoner." Later, asked why he had turned himself in, Frank replied simply: "I was tired of an outlaw's life."

Frank was taken by train to Independence, Missouri. Wherever the train stopped, people thronged about, hoping to get a look at the famous bandit. At Independence, he was greeted by a large crowd that included his mother, his wife, and his teenage son, Robert.

While Frank was in jail in Independence, two charges against him were dropped for lack of evidence. Then, in August, 1883, he was brought to trial in Gallatin, Missouri for the murder of Frank McMillan, the passenger killed during the Winston hold-up. The trial was held not in the county court house, which was too small to handle all the people who wanted to attend, but in the Gallatin Opera House. It was quite a show, and it ran for eight days before capacity crowds.

The most important prosecution witness was Dick Liddil, but Liddil, a horsethief and murderer, was open to the suspicion of selling Frank out to gain a pardon. Frank himself—mild, quiet-voiced, somewhat stooped—seemed very little like a ruthless outlaw. Another prosecution witness, a minister named Machette, pointed out Frank as one of two men who ate a meal at his home on the day before the robbery and described his ability to quote Shakespeare. It was a damning piece of testimony, since Frank's knowledge of the playwright's works was legendary.

The defense attempted to establish an alibi for Frank, claiming that he was staying with relatives at the time of the robbery. Frank's lawers also brought in General Jo Shelby, a Confederate war hero, to speak on Frank's behalf. The move almost backfired. Shelby staggered into the room so drunk he had to be guided to the witness chair, then rambled on in defiance of the judge's attempts to silence him. But Shelby's presence served to remind the jury of Frank's war record and of the familiar excuse that he had been driven to outlawry by Northerners. It took the jury three and a half hours to come to their decision. They found the defendent not guilty. Shortly afterward, several other charges against Frank were dropped because of legal technicalities.

In April, 1884 Frank stood trial for robbery in Huntsville, Alabama. His lawyers produced witnesses who swore that he had been in Nashville, Tennessee at the time the hold-up took place. Once again the jury brought back a verdict of not guilty.

But Frank was not yet in the clear. Still standing against him were charges connected with the Otterville hold-up. A trial was scheduled for February 23, 1885. It never took place. Two days before the trial date the charges were dismissed on the grounds that the prosecution's main witness had died.

Now, at last, with the remaining charges against him dropped or forgotten, Frank James was a free man. For the first time in twenty years he was no longer wanted by the law.

For the rest of his life Frank was a model of upright behavior.

He sold shoes; he herded horses; he worked as a doorman at a theater; he served as assistant starter at race tracks; he farmed; he acted in travelling shows. There was little evidence in his later years of the much-feared gunman he had once been.

At the time Frank went free, the Younger brothers were still imprisoned in Minnesota. Many attempts had been made to win them pardons. All had failed. Then, in 1889, Bob Younger died of tuberculosis. He had spent his last thirteen years in jail. Two years later, Jim and Cole Younger were released on parole but they were forbidden to leave the state. The following year, Jim, prevented from marrying a woman he loved because his legal rights had not been restored, was found dead in a St. Paul hotel room. He had shot himself in the head.

Not long afterward, Cole Younger was granted a full pardon and was allowed to return home to Missouri. For a short while he and Frank teamed up in a James-Younger Wild West Show in which Frank performed the part of a passenger in a mock stage-coach robbery. From time to time Cole gave church lectures on the theme: "Crime Does Not Pay." He, too, had come full circle.

Frank James died at the Samuel farm on February 18, 1915. Just over a year later, on March 21, 1916, Cole Younger died at his home in Lee's Summit, Missouri.

An era had come to an end.

CHAPTER FOURTEEN

The Legend of Jesse James

Of the countless stories told about Jesse James, many rely more on imagination than on fact. One that falls into this no man's land between history and myth is the tale of the weeping widow. Whether it is true or not seems almost beside the point. It is at the very heart of the James legend.

The story goes like this: Jesse and his gang were returning from a successful robbery, their wheat sack full of loot, when they stopped at a farmhouse for something to eat. The farm was owned by a widow, who agreed to prepare a meal for Jesse and his men. As she was getting the food ready, Jesse noticed tears in her eyes and asked what was wrong. The widow blurted out her tale. The farm was mortgaged, she said, and she was behind in her payments. The man who held the mortgage was coming that day, and unless she could pay him what she owed she would lose her home.

With a smile, Jesse told the widow that her problems were over. Reaching into the bulging wheat sack, he pulled out the money she needed. He warned her to take the mortgage note when she paid her debt so that she would have proof that the farm was hers. Then he asked her to describe the man in detail and to tell him exactly when he would be coming. After finishing their meal, Jesse and his men left, receiving the grateful thanks of the widow.

That afternoon, the mortgage-holder drove up in his buggy, expecting to take over the farm. To his amazement, the widow paid him in full, and he was forced to hand her the note of debt. Hidden from view, Jesse watched the man drive away from the farm. Then he and his companions came out from behind some bushes, took back the cash the man had just received, and went on their way.

In one version or another, this story has been widely repeated and widely believed. It forms the essence of the myth that Jesse was a kind of American Robin Hood who stole from the rich to give to the poor.

The myths about Jesse are attempts to explain or excuse a career of robbery and murder. He has been portrayed as the persecuted Confederate veteran, hunted relentlessly by his enemies and forced to become an outlaw. He has also been described as a champion of the poor against powerful banking and railroad interests. There is little truth in any of it.

Jesse James was a violent, ruthless marauder who stole what he refused to earn honestly and killed whoever stood in his way. He himself helped create and promote the myths that sought to excuse his lawlessness, and he used them to his advantage. On examination they prove flimsy. Beyond a few haphazard gestures of gallantry, which seem to have been staged for their calculated effect, there is no solid evidence that he used his illegal gains to benefit anyone but himself or that he discriminated in his choice of victims between rich and poor, male and female, Northerner and Southerner. Further, his claims that he was driven to outlawry have a strained ring of self-justification. Not all ex-guerrillas became bandits. Not everyone who opposed the excesses of the banks and the railroads challenged them with bullets. Jesse did.

There was a fresh wave of sympathy for Jesse following his

death. After all, he had been shot from behind by a traitor. The fact that he died uncaptured and untamed added to the peculiar romance of his story. He seemed beyond the rules that govern other men. He seemed bigger than life.

These were the beginnings of the legend. Its growth took many forms. There were songs and plays and dime novels and, later, films. As late as 1947 imposters stepped forth at regular intervals claiming that they were Jesse James. It was almost as though people believed that it would take more than a gun to kill him.

There were real contradictions in the man. He was at once sincerely religious and a blank-eyed killer. There is evidence of likeable qualities in him: humor, loyalty, shrewdness, and certainly bravery. A bit of a puritan, he neither drank nor smoked. He loved his children and his wife. But the fact that he was not in all respects a monster, leaves him far from being a hero. What talents he had, he used to victimize others. As Allan Pinkerton, head of the detective agency, remarked, he had "no more compunction about cold-blooded murder than he [had] about eating his breakfast."

Although Pinkerton was hardly an admirer of the Jameses, the evidence seems to support him. Jesse James was a thief and a killer. He became in legend what he never was in life.

Index